Teachers
Then and Now

Rob... .Ed.

D1261792

Contributing Author
Jill K. Mulhall, M.Ed.

Associate Editor
Christina Hill, M.A.

Assistant Editor
Torrey Maloof

Editorial Director
Emily R. Smith, M.A.Ed.

Project Researcher
Gillian Eve Makepeace

Editor-in-Chief
Sharon Coan, M.S.Ed.

Editorial Manager
Gisela Lee, M.A.

Creative Director
Lee Aucoin

Illustration Manager
Timothy J. Bradley

Designers
Lesley Palmer
Debora Brown
Zac Calbert
Robin Erickson

Project Consultant
Corinne Burton, M.A.Ed.

Publisher
Rachelle Cracchiolo, M.S.Ed.

Teacher Created Materials

5301 Oceanus Drive
Huntington Beach, CA 92649-1030
http://www.tcmpub.com
ISBN 978-0-7439-9375-3

Table of Contents

Changing Times

Teaching has changed over the years. Books are different. Classrooms do not look the same. Even the subjects we learn have changed. One thing has stayed the same, though. Teachers are important, and they change students' lives.

▲ This type of book was used long ago.

▲ These students know
the answer.

◄ A blind student reads
by feeling raised bumps
on a page.

The First Schools in America

Schools in the United States used to be one room. Students of all ages had the same teacher. Churches were in charge of many of the schools. Some parents did not want their children taught this way. So, they sent their children to **private schools**.

↓ A one-room school in Colorado

No school was free at that time. Parents had to pay whatever they could. Children of rich families did not go to the nearby schools. **Tutors** (TOO-terz) taught these children their lessons at home.

No Girls Allowed

Long ago, most girls did not get to go to school. Sometimes they went for a few years and then had to stop. People did not think girls needed to learn math or history. They thought only boys needed to study.

◀ Students of all ages used to learn in one room.

◆ This is a science class from over 100 years ago.

Teacher Education

The first teachers in the United States were not taught how to teach. They were just students who did well in school. They had to prove they could do the job. A **committee** (kuh-MIT-ee) tested them on reading and writing. That must have made them nervous (NER-vuhs). Most of them were only 14 or 15 years old! Later, teachers had to have more schooling. They had to get **degrees** (dih-GREEZ).

Today, teachers still have to get college degrees. They also take classes to learn how to teach.

Hey, Where's the Janitor?

At one time, teachers had to clean their classrooms. They had to sweep the floors and light fires in winter. It was part of their jobs.

↟ This teacher kept the fire going to warm his students.

Laura Ingalls ↓
stands with her sisters.

Laura Ingalls

Laura Ingalls was born in 1867. Her family moved around a lot. They were called **pioneers** (PI-uh-neerz). These were people who moved west in search of new land. Ms. Ingalls went to a one-room school. She loved school. She became a teacher when she was only 15 years old! When she grew up, she decided to write books about her childhood. These books are still read today.

Male and Female Teachers

Today, most teachers are women. It was not always this way. Long ago, most teachers in the United States were men. Then, people began to think that women were better with children. Also, women asked for less pay. Men moved on to other jobs. The same thing happened in many parts of the world.

Some people believe that more teachers should be men. They think students need to see how both **genders** (JEN-derz) should act.

⬇ This teacher helps her students.

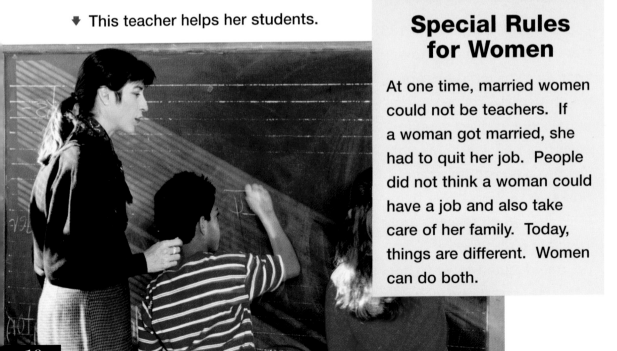

Special Rules for Women

At one time, married women could not be teachers. If a woman got married, she had to quit her job. People did not think a woman could have a job and also take care of her family. Today, things are different. Women can do both.

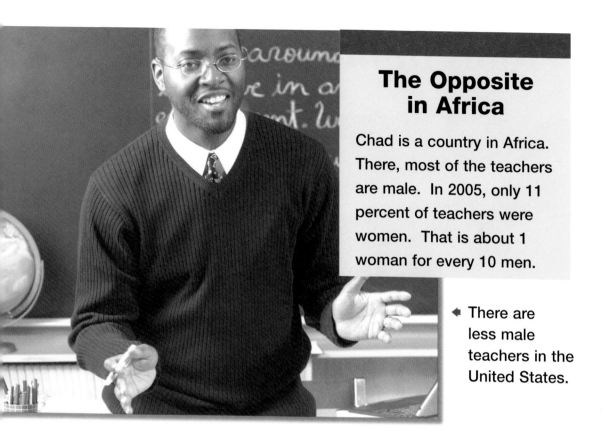

The Opposite in Africa

Chad is a country in Africa. There, most of the teachers are male. In 2005, only 11 percent of teachers were women. That is about 1 woman for every 10 men.

◄ There are less male teachers in the United States.

Percentage of Male Teachers in the United States from 1961–2001

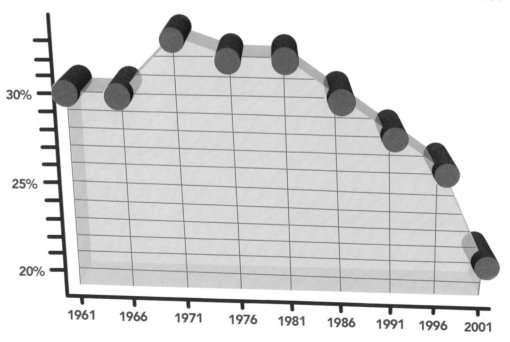

Tools in the Classroom

Slates Have Changed

There are some students in Kenya (KEH-nyuh), Africa, who use eSlates. These are tiny handheld computers. Students do not write on them, but read them like books. A large computer sends new information to the eSlates each day.

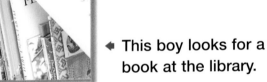

◄ This boy looks for a book at the library.

Two hundred years ago, there were few books in the classrooms. Students had to share. Books cost too much to have libraries. Students wrote on **slates** because paper was hard to find. If they did have paper, they used special pens. The pens had to be dipped in ink to write. It could get very messy!

Now, students have no problem finding books to read. Schools have libraries with many choices. Many classrooms even have computers to help students learn.

American hornbook ➤

A Book from a Bull

Long ago, children used a hornbook to learn to read. It was not actually a book. It was a flat board. A piece of paper was glued to the board. The hornbook had the alphabet and a prayer on it. A clear top sheet covered the writing to protect it. The top sheet was made from a bull's horn. This is why it was called a *horn*book.

◆ Students using computers

Teaching Behavior

Teachers are important **role models** in the lives of students. They show students the right way to act. Students learn skills that will make them good **citizens** (SIT-uh-zinz).

Teachers also help students get along with others. Children fight and argue. So, they need to learn how to solve problems. Teachers help them with this. They show students how to respect others.

⬇ Students learn the Pledge of Allegiance in a classroom in 1899.

▲ Students in Japan

Bullying in Japan

Schools in Japan have problems with bullies. Students who are different stand out. They get bullied. Japanese (jap-uh-NEEZ) teachers get special training on how to help solve this problem. Some teachers in the United States also get this training.

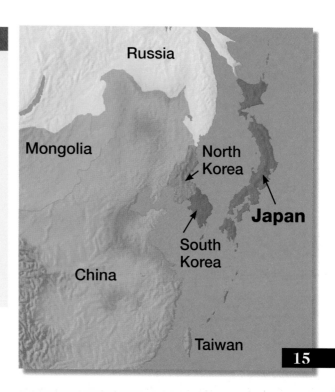

Russia

Mongolia

North Korea

China

South Korea

Japan

Taiwan

◀ Students sing in a music class.

These boys learned ▶
to work with wood
in class.

Different Kinds of Teachers

In the past, one teacher taught the whole school. Now, students get a new teacher every year. In middle school and high school, students have a teacher for each **subject**. It seems odd at first. Some students have six teachers a day. In college, students have many teachers, too. Each class has a different teacher. In college, teachers are called **professors** (pruh-FESS-uhrz).

Teachers are not just found at schools. Some teachers come to students' homes. Some even teach over the Internet!

Teaching English

Japan, China, and Spain are countries that want English teachers. English is spoken across the world. People in other countries want to learn it.

Tutors Today

Tutors may work at schools or students' homes. Some tutors teach children in hospitals. Tutors can teach all kinds of subjects. Or, they can just help students study for big tests. There are tutors who teach special things, like music and art. Some teach only one student at a time. This can be helpul for a lot of students.

⬇ These children paint pictures in an art class.

Homeschooling

Before there were schools, students learned at home. Now, many parents are teaching at home again. Would you like your mother or father to be your teacher?

Some parents **homeschool** because of their **religions** (rih-LIJ-uhnz). Others feel that their children learn better at home.

These students get a lot of attention. They never have to wait for anyone else!

A Homeschooled Genius

Thomas Edison was an inventor. He invented a new kind of light bulb. When he was a young boy, he had a hard time in school. He went to a one-room school for 12 weeks. He did not do very well. So, his parents decided to teach him at home. They also taught him how to use the library. That is how Edison learned about science. He owes his success to his parents.

⬇ Thomas Edison

Homeschool Capital of the World

The United States has the most homeschooled students. More than one million kids learn at home. Many communities have special groups for these children. They go on field trips together. They even have sports teams.

This sister ➡ reads a book to her brother.

◆ Teachers work hard to help their students learn.

Working as a Teacher Today

In some ways, teaching today is harder than it was long ago. Teachers have so much to teach in one year. They must teach a long list of **standards** (STAN-derdz). The standards are different for each grade level. In the past, teachers only had to teach the basics. If students could read, write, and do simple math, that was enough.

Today, teaching is easier in some ways, too. Teachers have more **resources** (reh-SORS-uhz) to help them reach students. Also, students are grouped by age. And, most class sizes are smaller.

Standards in Norway

All teachers in Norway follow the same teaching plans. This means that all students in Norway learn the same things. In the United States, each state decides its own standards.

⬆ This teacher helps her students in a computer lab.

⬇ Classroom in Afghanistan

Class Size Differences

In Italy (IT-uh-lee), the **average** (AV-uhr-ij) class had 11 students in 2002. In Afghanistan (af-GAN-uh-stan), the average class had 61 students. That's like two classes in the United States!

Still Growing

Will teaching keep changing? It looks that way. It has been happening for years. There are more tools for teachers now. There are also more demands. Today, there are many different ways to teach. Teachers have to choose which style works best for their students.

◄ A class learns about wool on a field trip.

Boys in a science lab ➨

▲ These students love to draw.

Teachers have very important jobs. Teaching is a job for people who enjoy learning. Teachers enjoy helping others. It is a career for those who want to make a difference.

A Day in the Life Then

Anne Sullivan (1866–1936)

Anne Sullivan (SUHL-uh-vuhn) had an illness as a child. It left her almost blind. But, she worked very hard in school. She graduated (GRAD-juh-wait-uhd) from college. Then, she decided to be a teacher. Her student was a little

▲ Helen Keller (left) with Anne Sullivan (right)

girl named Helen Keller. Helen could not hear, see, or speak. But, Ms. Sullivan was a very good teacher. She found ways to teach Helen.

Let's pretend to ask Anne Sullivan some questions about her job.

Why did you decide to be a teacher?

When I was a child, I couldn't read or write.

But, I really wanted to learn. When I was 14 years old, I was given the chance to go to school. My teachers helped me learn. It changed my life. I knew that I wanted to help other students learn. So, I became a teacher.

What is your day like?

I teach Helen new words every day. We walk around the house and the garden. When Helen touches an item, I spell the word for it in her hand. This is how she learns. We do this all day.

What do you like most about your job?

When I first became Helen's teacher, she could not speak to her family. Now, she can. I love that I have changed her life. That is why I like being a teacher.

⬆ Helen Keller (left) and Anne Sullivan (middle) sit with Alexander Graham Bell. Bell invented the telephone.

Tools of the Trade Then

This teacher wrote on a chalkboard. She taught the students to write in cursive (KUHR-siv). The chalkboard was an important tool.

This tool is called an abacus (AH-buh-kuhs). Students used it to practice math.

A classroom was a very important tool for teachers. This is a classroom from long ago. It probably looks different from your classroom today.

Long ago, there were no televisions. There were no DVD players. Teachers showed movies using film projectors (pruh-JEK-tuhrz).

Tools of the Trade Now

Many classrooms today use whiteboards instead of chalkboards. This student is practicing her math on the whiteboard.

↟ This is an LCD projector. Teachers can use LCD projectors for many lessons.

Today, students practice math with calculators. ➡

These students are using computers ➡ in a classroom. Computers can be helpful teaching tools.

A Day in the Life Now

Terence Ngo

Terence Ngo (TAIR-uhnts NO) is a teacher at Bonita (bo-NEE-tuh) Canyon Elementary School. He teaches sixth grade. His favorite sport is soccer. He likes to teach kids how to play soccer after school.

Why did you decide to become a teacher?

I love kids. And, I love to learn! I wanted to become a teacher so I could work with kids. I like making an impact on students. I knew that I wanted to become a teacher in my second year of college. That was the first time I coached soccer. I will always remember the smiles on the faces of those kids.

What is your day like?

My day is busy, busy, busy! Every day is different. It depends on the mood of the class. I always have lessons planned. My students complete each lesson. Together, we learn new things. During my day, I also spend time with other teachers. We plan lessons.

After school you can find me on the soccer field. There, I spend time coaching the sport that I love!

What do you like most about your job?

I love working with students. Every day brings new challenges. I like seeing my students learn. This makes my job fun! It is also great to be a role model for students.

Glossary

average—the middle number

citizens—people who live in a community

committee—a group of people who work together to do a job

degrees—titles given when people complete their studies at college

genders—one of two groups, male or female

homeschool—to teach children in the home instead of sending them to school

pioneers—early settlers in America

private schools—schools that are not run by the government

professors—teachers at college

religions—groups that service and worship together

resources—stocks and supplies

role models—people others look up to and want to act like

slates—hard boards that students wrote on with chalk and could erase

standards—skills that all students in a grade must learn

subject—topic of learning, such as science or history

tutors—people paid to teach only certain children

Index

Credits

Acknowledgements

Special thanks to Terence Ngo for providing the *Day in the Life Now* interview. Mr. Ngo is a teacher in Irvine, California.

Image Credits

cover Eyewire; p.1 Eyewire; p.4 The Granger Collection, New York; pp.4–5 Photodisc; p.5 Photodisc; p.6 Denver Public Library; p.7 The Granger Collection, New York; p.8 The Library of Congress; p.9 (top) The Granger Collection, New York; p.9 (bottom) The Granger Collection, New York; p.10 Photodisc; p.11 (top) Ablestock; p.11 (bottom) Tim Bradley, illustrator; p.12 Photos.com; p.13 (top) The Granger Collection, New York; p.13 (bottom) Photodisc; p.14 The Library of Congress; p.15 (top) Maryanne Russell/Time Life Pictures/Getty Images; p.15 (bottom) Lesley Palmer/Digital Wisdom; p.16 (left) Eyewire; p.16 (right) The Library of Congress; p.17 Eyewire; p.18 The Library of Congress; p.19 (top) iStockphoto.com/Maartje van Caspel; p.19 (bottom) Hemera Technologies, Inc.; p.20 Photodisc; p.21 (top) Comstock; p.21 (bottom) Paula Bronstein/Getty Images; p.22 (left) Photodisc; p.22 (right) Photodisc; p.23 PhotoCreate/Shutterstock, Inc.; p.24 The Library of Congress; p.25 The Granger Collection, New York; p.26 (top) The Library of Congress; p.26 (center right) Photos.com; p.26 (center left) ChipPix/Shutterstock, Inc.; p.26 (bottom) Clipart.com; p.27 (top left) iStockphoto.com/Scott Dunlap; p.27 (top right) iStockphoto.com/John Archer; p.27 (bottom left) Jaimie Duplass/Shutterstock, Inc.; p.27 (bottom right) Photos.com; p.28 Courtesy of Terence Ngo; p.29 Courtesy of Terence Ngo; back cover The Library of Congress